PATRICK WOODHOUSE

With you is the well of life

Prayers from the depths of the heart

kevin mayhew

First published in 2005 by

KEVIN MAYHEW LTD
Buxhall, Stowmarket, Suffolk, IP14 3BW
E-mail: info@kevinmayhewltd.com

9 8 7 6 5 4 3 2 1 0

ISBN 1 84417 380 1
Catalogue No. 1500784

Cover design by Jonathan Stroulger
Edited by Marian Reid
Typeset by Fiona Connell Finch

Contents

Patrick Woodhouse is Canon Precentor of Wells Cathedral where he has oversight of the cathedral's liturgy and music. Before moving to Wells he was the Vicar of St Andrew's Chippenham in Wiltshire, and before that he worked in the Church of England's ministry of social responsibility as Adviser in the Dioceses of Carlisle and Winchester. He is author of *In Search of the Kingdom* (Marshall Pickering, 1989) and *Beyond Words: an introduction, guide and resource for a contemplative way of prayer* (Kevin Mayhew, 2001). He is married to Sam, an education adviser, and they have two grown-up daughters.

Introduction

The Well – A Symbol of New Life

Anyone who has spent any time living in parts of the world where there is no piped water will know how important the well is in any community. Morning and evening, women of a village will come to the well to meet and to draw up water from deep in the ground for their crops, their animals, and their homes. In such communities the well is the source of life, both physically, as without its precious water life would be impossible, and spiritually, for the well brings the community together. At the well, people meet, exchange news, share concerns, tell stories, drink, and collect life-giving water to share with others. Here relationships develop and are strengthened day by day. At the well, love may be born. At the well, meetings take place which lead to new life and new futures. The well is a place of encounter – and infinite possibility.

This is also true in both the Old and the New Testaments. Early in the Old Testament an encounter takes place at a well which leads to the beginning of Israel's life as a people. Abraham's servant, who has been sent to find a wife for Abraham's son Isaac, sees Rebecca coming to draw water at the well at the city of Nahor. There is a long and lovely story of how he asks her for water and eventually he takes her back to be Isaac's wife. It is one of the founding relationships of the people of God, for from Isaac and Rebecca, Jacob who was to become Israel, is born. And then Jacob in his turn meets Rachel at a well, and from them the twelve tribes of Israel come into being, and the nation is born.

In the New Testament, early in the Gospel of John, there is also a most significant meeting place at a well. Jesus, who at the wedding feast at Cana in Galilee has been revealed as the true, though secret bridegroom, meets a woman at the well of Sychar – a woman whom John the Evangelist, by placing this story at this point in his Gospel, is suggesting represents his bride. She is a lonely, exhausted, and thirsty figure, and a foreigner – a despised Samaritan. Her life is chaotic and immoral, and within her own community of women she is being ostracised, for she draws water alone in the middle of the day. And yet as she talks with this stranger about thirst, and water from the well, and 'living water' drawn from the depths of the human heart, he gently reveals himself to her, as she does to him, in a mutual unveiling of who each of them truly is. It is an extraordinarily beautiful and even intimate meeting full of acceptance, understanding and surprise. She becomes the first person in the Gospel to learn his true identity – the Messiah of God, and to hear words from him that speak of the ancient name of God – I am. As she leaves her water-jar, symbolising the burdens she has carried from which she is now released, and runs to the town, overwhelmed and barely believing what has happened both *to* her and *within* her, she becomes, we may say, the first evangelist.

So in the Bible the well is a place of huge significance symbolising the fertile life-giving power of God. It is a symbol worth reflecting on in the particular time and world we now live in, for it points to aspects and possibilities of spiritual experience that all too often are ignored – particularly in the churches.

Spiritual Attitudes That Are Counter-Cultural

In a society overwhelmed by the speed of change, in which anxiety and insecurity are rampant and play havoc with the capacity of human beings to relate well to one another, the symbol of the well speaks of our need to attend to spiritual attitudes that run counter to the prevailing culture.

It reminds us of our need to be concerned not so much with instant communication, but rather the dimension of depth in human relationships; not so much with rapid mobility as the capacity to be still; not so much with immediate answers as the need to wait; not so much with the satisfaction of superficial desire, as the hard work of entering into the peace 'which passes all understanding'. In the midst of a popular culture obsessed with what is external, superficial and ephemeral, the well as a symbol of where the divine life may be found points to the challenge of exploring the hidden source of life in the depths of the human heart. It may be likened to digging for water in an arid and parched landscape where there appears to be none.

It is with this dimension of *depth*, of longings and desires that lie *within* at the most profound level, that these prayers are concerned. They touch upon universal human themes: our need for understanding and acceptance, our hunger for belonging and friendship, our restless search for meaning, and the sense, inarticulate but persistent within all of us, that our time on earth is a journey, even a pilgrimage towards something infinitely greater. Above all, the prayers seek to evoke something of the need apparent in all cultures and under many forms to bow down, to worship and to adore the mystery of the Creator, who in the Christian story is also Redeemer and Saviour.

Though conceived and written in the context of Christian worship, and often in response to Christian texts, it is my hope that in addition to helping church members these prayers may be of help to those who find church membership difficult. Those many people, both within and outside the churches, who while they feel they cannot share any confident expressions of committed belief yet feel the need for a living spirituality.

Working in one of England's finest cathedrals where we receive huge numbers of visitors every year, we are very conscious of the needs of such people. People who, despite the rampant secular ideology of a post-Christian society which constantly asserts that God is dead, discover that they cannot altogether escape the notion of God. People who become aware, in all sorts of circumstances in their lives, of hints, intuitions and glimpses that suggest the reality of the Divine. People who, even though they may have difficulty in belonging as fully fledged members of a church, nevertheless feel that life cannot be fully lived without a transcendent dimension. People in short who long to pray even while they find the words that the church so often uses, difficult. These prayers are written with such people in mind, as well as regular church members who seek a greater depth in their spirituality. They aim to resonate with a kind of questioning longing as well as to take people deeper towards the Source of that longing.

Wells Cathedral

There is a more personal reason for choosing the symbol of the well for the title of this collection, and for thinking of prayer in terms of the hard work of drawing water from a great depth.

The cathedral where I work at Wells at the foot of the Mendip Hills in Somerset takes its name from ancient wells which still bubble up close to the cathedral's east end. Indeed the wells are the reason a cathedral stands on this spot. There is evidence that from ancient times people have come down to the foot of the hills in this place, to find life-giving water. It is a symbol we are constantly aware of and seek to make use of in our liturgy.

However, the water of the wells at Wells is not a silent pool at a great depth down to which a bucket has to be patiently lowered. Rather the wells evoke much more the idea in John's Gospel, Chapter Four, of 'living water welling up to eternal life'. For that is the kind of wells they are – gushing springs that pour out clear water from the depths. Still to this day thousands of litres an hour gush up a mere few yards from the cathedral Lady Chapel.

It is an ever constant reminder of the never ending love of God that the cathedral in its daily worship and community life seeks to receive, to celebrate and to proclaim.

Style and Structure of These Prayers: Abiding in God, Seeking His Kingdom

Most of the prayers in this collection were written for use at Cathedral Evensong which is the principal moment of public worship in our daily life. They are essentially contemplative in style as all deepest prayer must be – not striving after what *we* want, but aiming to help us rest in the mystery of God and to see and seek his purposes in the world he came to save. And that dual aim has dictated the book's structure.

The first half entitled 'Prayers of Abiding in the Love of God' is made up of prayers whose aim is to help people rest or 'abide', to use one of the favourite words from the Gospel of John, where Christ bids us 'abide' in him. This is the first hugely challenging task in the life of prayer. The challenge of learning to be still and rest in God, allowing the chattering restless mind gently to descend into the stillness of the heart and there drink from the water of the Spirit welling up for eternal life. This is the focus of the first half.

But learning to be still and centred in God is not enough. We need to move out into the world. So the book leads in the second half into 'Prayers of Seeking the Kingdom of God'. These prayers aim to move those who pray, in mind and imagination, out into God's struggling suffering world and help them offer their concern and longing that God's Kingdom of justice and peace may come.

Dotted about among the prayers, which cover a wide range of issues and concerns and for ease of use are simply placed in alphabetical order, are prayers in thanksgiving for the lives of the saints. Just a few of the principal saints of the calendar have been chosen. Praying about them reminds us that the Christian faith is never a kind of abstract set of beliefs, but is only ever known as it is incarnated – made flesh – in the lives of those who struggle in their particular time to remain faithful. There is no particular reason why some saints are the subject of thanksgiving and not others, merely that these saints are among those who have particularly caught my imagination and moved me to write about them as we have prayed our way at the cathedral through the seasons of the year. Readers might like to add to the book by writing their own prayer about their own particular favourite saint either from the past or from the present.

Prayers for Both Public and Private Use

While these prayers have been written for public worship, I hope that they may equally be used in private meditation. We need to deepen our practice of both – the public affirmation of the love of God amidst the chaos of the world's strivings, and the silent secret seeking of his face, in the depths of our own hearts.

A brief word about both these dimensions.

Public Prayer

Prayer in the context of public worship must always be more than just 'saying prayers'. Careful attention must be paid to some key ingredients if our praying is to embrace not just the mind but the heart also. In the next section I have spelt out specific guidelines for using the prayers in public worship – but first some general principles.

First, prayers in public worship must be allowed to 'breathe'. It is crucial that they are surrounded and punctuated by moments of silence and stillness. And if our praying is to resonate with levels of human experience deeper than the rational mind, then it is also important that the prayers are not rushed. People need time to centre down, to leave behind them the muddle and rush of their daily existence, and to enter into a deep place of stillness where they can address the hunger and need that lies hidden in their hearts.

Second, beware of too many words. This is a constant temptation for those who lead worship. We think we will be heard for our 'much speaking'. Moving from one topic to another with scarcely a pause in between, trying to fit in all the concerns of homes, neighbourhood and world is an exhausting and spiritually fruitless business. At the end of such a time of prayer people go away drained and empty. Keep to just a few prayers.

Third, think carefully about introductions. More about this is spelt out in the guidelines. The main thing is to make linkages – with the readings, with the psalms – and in cathedrals or churches where there is a strong choral tradition, with the anthem especially. Such can be the power of choral music that it can take people to a place in the depths of their hearts which is beyond words, and that is what the prayers aim to do. So moving from sung words to spoken words, it makes sense to build on what has gone before so enabling people to abide and go deeper into the love of God into which the music has led them. Many of the prayers in this collection were inspired by the text of anthems, or by a text from the New or Old Testament, and so occasionally that text is printed in italics at the top of the page. It can be read aloud as a way into the prayer itself.

Private Prayer

I hope these prayers will also be an encouragement in the practice of private prayer. I have written on this elsewhere and I will not attempt to summarise that book here (*Beyond Words: an introduction, guide and resource for a contemplative way of prayer*, Kevin Mayhew, 2001).

I would simply want to say that although private prayer is above all an adventure into silence – always the first language of God – written prayers can have their place too when you 'go into your room and shut the door and pray to your Father in secret'. But they should be used sparingly and slowly, always paying regard to silence and preparation of heart and mind before diving into them. As you pray them, aloud or in silence, let your mind linger over or quietly repeat any word or phrase that particularly captures your attention. That way you will be taking the meanings you find in the text down below the level of your rational mind into the depths of your heart where the Holy Spirit of God can use them to do his silent work of healing and directing your concern that his will be done in the world.

Finally, while learning to pray – finding the 'narrow way' into the joy of God – is the most important thing we shall ever do in our lives, it is worth adding that it is never easy.

For all prayer – whether private or public – is a struggle. A struggle to wake up from our blindness and neglect, and to *see* – to see what is real. A struggle to break out of the illusions which we weave around our minds, so hiding us from the reality of the God who is trying to reach us, and break through to a deeper dimension of life where we discover not division and multiplicity, fear and competition, but an extraordinary oneness. A oneness with the One whom we recognise is the source of all our life, and the end of all our desires; a oneness with our truest and deepest selves as we discover his buried neglected image deep in our hearts; a oneness with and between one another, both in the community of faith and more widely in the world he loves and came to save.

Guidelines

for Using This Book in Public Worship

1. Choosing Prayers

The best guide to the content of the prayers is given in their titles. In order to know which to turn to in the planning of worship, it is worth spending time carefully reading through them, praying them in private, and becoming familiar with them. As a result of such familiarity you may care to construct your own simple index.

There are two indices at the back of the book – of subjects and of seasons, indicating which prayers may be particularly helpful for a particular issue or at a particular season. It is a rough guide only and not inclusive of every subject referred to in the prayers.

2. Introducing Prayers

How a prayer is introduced can be as important as the prayer itself. Good liturgy is about helping people make connections, so in a simple and brief introduction the meanings in the readings or the psalms or the anthem can be picked up – with the prayer therefore becoming the vehicle of their offering.

Another way of introduction is for the person leading the worship to pick up an issue from the news or to refer to a concern in the worshipping community, and use these to lead into the prayer. This kind of connecting helps people experience an overall *coherence*. If ideas and themes and meanings are gathered together and sensitively offered, people have the sense that the longings of their hearts have been satisfied, the burdens of their concerns have been laid down, and they can rest in the confidence that God is with them, and has heard.

But beware of being verbose. Introductions should do no more than evoke a theme, and not be sermons in disguise. A few well-crafted words are sufficient, followed by a brief pause, and then the prayer.

3. Praying Prayers

Praying is far more than reading words of prayers. To pray is to do an extraordinary thing. It is to seek to be silent and still (and in our restless pressured world that is demanding enough) and enter into the presence of God, and there, in the spaciousness of his accepting love, to articulate the deepest longings of people's hearts. Aware of the immensity of this calling, those who lead prayers need to tread gently, allowing time for words to breathe.

The prayers in this book are deliberately set out on the page with space around them in order to evoke a sense of spaciousness in God. In praying them try to find a right balance between words and silence, and to be sensitive to the length of pauses and the pace of sentences. As a guide to this the prayers have been written with gaps in the text, and careful punctuation to indicate pauses.

However, while it is most important not to rush, it is also important not to be too ponderous and burden words with more emotion than they can carry. The rule is to let the meanings in the prayers dictate both the pace and how the prayers are prayed, meanings that need to be sensed, discovered and known, in the heart of the one who prays.

4. Limiting the Number of Prayers

Leading a time of prayer may be likened to serving a good meal. Don't offer too much so that your guests have indigestion or simply cannot take any more. If you have chosen your prayers carefully, if they have been introduced well, if they have been surrounded by appropriate silences, then three or four will probably be quite sufficient.

At Evensong at Wells Cathedral the normal pattern is to begin the time of prayer with a prayer that evokes praise or picks up a phrase from the anthem or simply enables people to 'abide' in the love of God. This 'abiding' is so important. We need to learn to rest deeply in God. In this collection, prayers such as 'Rest' or 'The cave of the heart' or 'In you alone is our peace' seek to take people into this contemplative rest. There then may follow a prayer that picks up a theme from one of the readings. Finally there may be one or two prayers of intercession that look outward to the concerns and needs of the world.

This means that the prayer time is a kind of journey in itself leading the worshipper out from a sense of stillness and beauty and abiding, into the concerns and needs of the world God loves. Finally, it is best to end the time of prayer with a period of silence during which people may offer their own particular concerns, and everything may be gathered up finally in the words of the grace.

Of course the situation will be different in different contexts. Prayer time in a cathedral will be different from a church where the congregation know each other well, or a house group where the praying is less formal. But whatever the situation it is important to recognise the limits of people's capacity for attention in the hard work of prayer so that they go away not oppressed – and listening to someone else praying can easily become oppressive – but rather thankful and uplifted and blessed.

One:

Prayers of Abiding in the Love of God

Adoration

In the adoration of God
we find our true selves,
the buried, forgotten,
image of God within.

We adore you
most glorious God.
Through your Son Jesus Christ
your love shines out,
your Spirit is given,
and the light of your kingdom
dawns in our darkness.

As we bless your holy name
in the depths of hearts grown still,
free us from the power of
the world's illusions
and the temptations of
the ego's false trail.

And gazing
on the cross of your Son,
open our eyes
to love's freedom;

our hearts
to love's pain;

our souls
to love's joy.

So shall we know who we are,
and live,

for your glory.

Amen.

As a deer longs for flowing streams

As a deer longs for flowing streams,
so longs my soul for you, O God.
Psalm 42:1

In the silence and beauty
of this house of prayer
we offer you ourselves,
O God,
in all our complexity and need.

You know the longings of our hearts;
our hunger for acceptance,
our need for understanding,
our search for recognition,
our desire for love;

As a deer longs for flowing streams,
so longs my soul for you, O God.

O God,
you are the Lover of Souls,
the root and spring of all grace;
look with compassion
on the arid emptiness of our lives,

and teach us what it means to desire you
not just through the restrained formalities of religion
but with the passionate intensity of a thirsty animal.

And when we find you,
elusive God,
give us to drink from that well of life
which gushes up like a living stream
from the heart of Jesus Christ,

who is our Life,
our Love,
and our Lord.

Amen.

Barnabas

Today we celebrate the Feast of Barnabas.

Comforting Spirit of God
we bless you for your apostle Barnabas,
'son of encouragement',
who broke down barriers of mistrust
and ignoring fear,
took hold of the hand of Saul
and brought him into the community of the apostles.

As we rejoice in his quiet strength
we bless you for all those who
in our lives
with gentle persistence
and patient courage
have dissolved our cynicism,
dismantled our fear,
and warmed and widened our hearts;

and so have been to us
messengers of Christ.

Make us too,
we pray,
men and women of encouragement;

that in the light of our lives
belief may live again,
and fear be conquered.

In the power of Jesus Christ,

Amen.

Contradictions

In the silence of this holy place we offer you,
O God,
the contradictions of our lives:

our emptiness,
and moments when we recognise
goodness overflowing;

our lostness,
and the knowledge
too deep for words
that we are found;

our arrogance,
when we blunder around blindly,
not knowing what we are doing,
and then wake up to our need;

our loneliness,
and the momentary intuition
that somehow
we deeply belong;

our restlessness,
and the gift of finding rest
in your acceptance;

O Spirit of God,
in the confused perplexity of who we are,
keep us ever moving forward
in search of your grace;

and as we travel,
deepen our stillness,
and focus our longing;
that alive to your comforting Spirit
we may grow in the way of holiness,
and become the redeemed people
of your love.

In Christ our Lord.

Amen.

Crying in the wilderness

The voice of one crying in the wilderness . . .
Luke 3:4

God our Saviour,
as John cried out
in the barren wastes of Judea
so do I cry.

In the noise and rush
of my crowded life
I run from you,
and most days
in my empty busyness
manage to avoid you.

In your mercy
show me the silent path I must take
to the wilderness of my heart's longing;
and give me courage
to face my need.

O God,
stillness, and silence
frighten me.

I do not know what to do.

Show me in my fragility
that it is in my emptiness
that the rose will blossom;

and that it will be
from the dry ground of my longing
that the water of life will spring;

for you are my God,
and my hope,
for ever.

Amen.

Dedication

At the dedication of the temple he had built
King Solomon prayed:

*'May your eyes be open day and night towards this house,
the place where you promised to set your name.'*
1 Kings 8:29

We kneel in silence and adoration,
and bless you
Lord our God
for the beauty of this house of prayer.

We bless you for all who have loved
and adorned it over the centuries,
and have,
through its very fabric,
in art and sculpture,
wood and stone,
glass and paint,
ironwork and needlework,
told the story of the gospel.

Make us worthy in our time
to care for all this beauty;

that eyes grown blind may see again,
minds grown dull may awake again,
and hearts grown cold may be warmed again
in the vision of your loveliness;

for your glory's sake.

Amen.

Francis of Assisi

Whoever does not receive
the Kingdom of God as a child
will never enter it.
Luke 18:17

We bless God for Francis
the little poor man of Assisi
whose joy and humility in Christ
lit up the medieval world,
and who showed what it means to be childlike,
in delight and praise.

Childlike God
set your pilgrim people free
from the burdens of self-importance we carry,
the masks of pomposity we hide behind.

Father,
as we grow older,
show us how to grow younger,
until we become again
like little children
in simplicity, trust and joy;

and like the Blessed Francis
offer you hearts
full of nothing
but praise.

Amen.

Friendship

In the Gospel of John, Jesus Christ says:
'I do not call you servants any longer, I call you friends' (John 15:15).

We bless you
O Lord our God
for the gift of friendship,
in our homes, our families,
and the life of this community.

For friendships
kindled in laughter,
shared in work,
celebrated in faith,
discovered in grief,
strengthened in sorrow,
sealed in forgiveness,
deepened in the intimacy of love.

And we especially bless you for those friendships that,
like slender bridges slung across the dark valleys
of our fear and self-doubt,
have reached into our alienation,
touched our despair,
healed us of our loneliness,
and made us one.

Sustain and deepen us,
O God,
in our friendships;

for in the delight of shared lives
we see your joy,
and in the acceptance
of mutual vulnerability
we know your Son,

Jesus Christ,
who is Saviour
and Lord of all.

Amen.

Gratitude

As we reflect on the story of our lives,
we bless you
life-giving God
for those moments
when gratitude,
like light in darkness
has burst upon us
taking us by surprise;

moments when we thought we were forgotten,
and found we were recognised;

when we thought we were alone,
and found we were understood;

when we were afraid,
and found our fear was an illusion;

when we thought we lived in a world without meaning,
and found meaning strangely given;

when we thought death was the end,
and then, in the face of death,
found ourselves moved to believe in Life.

Give us always
a grateful heart,
O God,

and keep us ever alert
to the surprise of your coming,
in Jesus Christ our Lord.

Amen.

Hope

Risen Christ,
who went before your disciples
into Galilee of the Gentiles,
Galilee of the wide world,
and who calls us to follow you,
like Abraham,
into the unknown
with the promise of a new future,
kindle
we pray
within our fragile hearts
your precious gift of hope,
and the courage to believe and work for
that day when,
despite all things
which again and again betray hope,
all will be well,
and all manner of things shall be well;
for you are our God
whose purpose of love
cannot fail.

Amen.

House of prayer

When Jesus of Nazareth walked into the noisy chaos
of the Temple in Jerusalem with a whip of cords,
he fiercely insisted that it be a house of prayer.
Luke 19:45–6

Teach us
O God
to hallow this place,
our temple,
as a holy place
day by day.

May here
the lonely find comfort,
the fearful – reassurance,
the anxious – calm,
the despairing – hope,
the guilty – forgiveness,
the lost – direction,
and the desperate
the freedom and peace they long for.

Father,
as day by day
we adore your holy name
lead us gently,
we pray,
from the confusions of the world
into the still spaces of our hearts' longing;
and open the way
in the depths of our souls
to the springs of your life.

In the name of Christ
our Lord.

Amen.

In you alone is our peace

God our Maker,
whose Spirit broods over our chaos
and whose love enters it;
teach us in this holy place
to breathe again.

In your mercy
lead us away from
the distractions
and clamour of our hearts' confusion
into that still abiding place
where in you,
O Christ,
our life begins;

and we glimpse
in the depths of our souls' yearning
the light of heaven.

For in you alone is our peace
who are Father, Son and Holy Spirit
in love abiding,
evermore,

Amen.

Joy

O be joyful in the Lord
Psalm 100

O God, in this season of Easter / Pentecost / Trinity
(on this festival day)
you offer us the gift of joy.
And yet so often we cannot receive it.
Our lives seem out of joint,
dislocated,
at odds with others and ourselves,
harassed,
and hurt,
and hurting.

In our frustration
all we know is the cry of the exiles who hung up their harps
beside the waters of Babylon
and lamented:
'How can we sing the Lord's song in a strange land?'

Yet you command us to be joyful
as you are joyful.

Our confidence,
O God, our life,
is that your joy,
bursting everywhere through the fabric
of the greening world
is greater than all our walled-up fear,
our anger,
our tired despair.

Be patient with us
gentle, joyful God;
and lead us from the bleak desert of our need
to the sweet paradise of your praise,
and release in us
the gift,
the song
of joy.

Amen.

Lamb of God

Agnus Dei,
Lamb of God,
dumb before your shearers
Son of God,

we worship you.

Lamb of God,
self-offering Man of God,
embracing a world
estranged from God,

we worship you.

Lamb of God,
pain-bearing Man of God,
companion in despair
to all alone from God,

we worship you.

Lamb of God,
one with God,
in heaven and hell
our only hope in God,

we worship you.

Lent

God,

Lent is a time for reality.
An end to the games,
the illusions,
the fabrications we feed off,
yet which betray us.

And in their place,
nothing but gazing
into the blank emptiness of a desert;
from where,
you promise,
life will come.

O God,
it is strange and frightening
if we dare enter it.
Space,
silence,
emptiness,
nothing but waiting.

Stones become loaves.
Heights, great platforms on which to be admired.
Rock, pinnacles of buildings to jump from.

The mind wanders,
flirting with the shadows of its fantasies.

Have mercy upon us

O Refiner.
O Purifier.
O Tester of hearts.

And shape our wayward souls too,
like his,
into instruments for the world's joy.

Amen.

Lives that offer life

One thing I have asked of the Lord,
one thing I seek:
to live in the house of the Lord
all the days of my life,
to behold the beauty of the Lord
and to inquire in his temple.

'Come,' my heart says, 'seek his face!'
Your face, Lord, do I seek.
Psalm 27:4, 8

God of life,
we bless you for the glory of this holy place;
and confess that in the presence of beauty
we find ourselves profoundly questioned.

Our lives seem shallow.

Skating along the surface of our days
we know we are hasty,
easily distracted,
and lack roots;

and in the giving of ourselves,
generosity.

Have mercy on us;
and by your Spirit
wake us up to our need;
and give us courage
to seek your face;

that grounded again in your being,
and rooted again in your silence,
we may bear amongst those around us

the rich fruit
of lives that offer the gift of life.

Amen.

Mary

We bless you,
O Lord our God,
for Mary of Nazareth;

who said 'let it be'
and became the God-bearer;

who magnified your name
in exultant joy;

who pondered the mystery of her child
as wise men worshipped;

who stood before Simeon
and heard that a sword would pierce her heart;

who waited in darkness
as priests jeered;

who rejoiced in wonder
in his risen Life.

Give us,
O God,
a faith like Mary's;

that risks and says yes,
that wonders in silence,
that trusts through pain,
that waits in darkness,
that exults in joy.

So may we too
in the midst of all that we face,
bear your life in our hearts,
and shine with the light of hope;

for your joy's sake.

Amen.

Our hearts' meaning

Alleluia.

We bless you,
O God of our life.

In the beginning you spoke,
and light came.

Breathing on chaos,
form emerged.

Taking hold of the dust of the ground,
human beings were created.

And then in Jesus Christ
you came among us:

blind eyes were opened,
deaf ears unstopped,
dull hearts ignited,

and a native innocence grew again
in the soul of humankind
and paradise was unlocked;
and like wondering children
we stepped into temples of your praise;
and making songs to your glory
found our hearts' meaning.

Alleluia.

We bless you,
O God of our life.

Amen.

Rest

Take from us
O Lord our God
all that hinders,
restricts,
and denies
the longing of our restless souls
to find their rest in you.

O silent Liberator of hearts that are besieged,
forgive our fearfulness,
calm our waywardness,
and deepen our attentiveness;

that with undistracted gaze
we may learn to look
upon the face of your adoring;
and in the embrace of Jesus Christ
find ourselves healed.

For your love's sake.

Amen.

Seeking the beauty of God

Today, as every day in this cathedral/church,
is a day of praise as we lift up our eyes
to seek the beauty of God:

Beauty in this holy place,
beauty in the play of light and shadow,
beauty in the form and shape of stone,
beauty in truth,
beauty in music,
beauty in silence,
beauty in art,
beauty in the face of the stranger.

Beauty in a crucified figure
who had no beauty.

O crucified God,
as we fill this place with your praise
save us from the worship that costs us nothing.

And as you have given us all things
in Jesus Christ,
teach us,
we pray,
the daily path of our surrender;

that in losing our life
we may find it;
in giving
we may receive it;

and in dying we may be reborn
to that new beauty
being shaped in us
by the power of your Spirit,
and through the love
of Jesus Christ
our Lord.

Amen.

Simeon

Mine eyes have seen thy salvation
which thou hast prepared in the sight of every peoples,
a light to lighten the Gentiles
and the glory of your people, Israel.
Luke 2:30

We bless you,
O Lord our God,
for old Simeon.

For the faithfulness of his watching,
the discipline of his praying,
and the persistence of his trust
that over the decades of his long vigil
had purified his soul,
opened his eyes,
and enabled him to see.

As we celebrate today
his gift of sight,
given in the still silence of the Temple,
look with your mercy upon us
who fail to see.

And teach us,
your blind wayward children,
how to find the same narrow way
that leads to your freedom.

That hearts entangled in passion,
minds shrouded in fear,
and souls distracted by need,
may be still;

and in the discipline of a purified life
may also see;

your face,
O God,
in the eyes of a child.

Amen.

The cave of the heart

Teach us,
O Christ,
the quiet way
down
into the silence
of hearts emptied
and grown still,
there to wait for your abiding.

As your Spirit
steals gently over the face
of our longing,
give,
we pray,
the gift of rest,
and a freedom from those compulsions
which drive us on
and cause again your passion.

Thus shall we know your
lightness of being;
and from the dark cave of our hearts
rise up
and live
a strong new day;

instruments of your peace
for the world's joy.

Amen.

The gift of music

Let us bless God for the gift of music.

O Christ,
whose birth was greeted with the song of angels,
whose mother sang as she magnified the Lord,
and who was greeted in the Temple by the song of Simeon,
we bless you for the gift of music.

For music
which calms our fears,
lifts our hearts,
speaks to our souls,
and takes us
beyond words,
into the presence of your joy.

Give us,
O Lord,
a deeper love for this language of your praise;

that in its light, we may see light,
and in its glory, find your glory,

O Christ our life,
our love,

our endless song.

Amen.

The gift of wisdom

God,
we are a confused
and driven people
overwhelmed with information,
saturated with knowledge,
and bombarded with distractions
in a culture that is empty,
bereft,
and searching.

Father,
amid our confusions
give us,
we pray,
your gift of wisdom.

As we learn
patiently
to abide in your holy fear,

may our seeing deepen to insight,
our thinking mature to understanding,
and our listening break through to love;

so,
led by your Spirit,
shall we find
in all the bewildering circumstances
of our times
that narrow way that leads to life,
trodden by him
who has gone before us into joy,

Jesus Christ,
our King.

Amen.

The glory of being human

*At its beginning and at its end all prayer
is a great shout of joy, a paean of praise
for the sheer miracle of existence,
and the glory of being human . . .*

Giver of Life,
we adore you
and bow before you.

You created the light of the sun in the morning
and this good earth beneath our feet;
you delighted in the myriad forms
emerging on the earth
and in the depths of the sea;

you laid out the expanse of the oceans,
wove the tapestry of the stars,
sculpted the beauty of the moon,
and spread out the vast space of this universe.

And in the end you created us
in the vulnerability of our smallness,
the frailty of our mortality,
and the potential of our glory.

You formed us in your image,
and gave us a heart to love you
and destined us for your likeness.

Lift up our eyes to the glory of our possibilities,
O beckoning God;
and teach us how to find
your secret beauty
hidden within us,
as we serve and love and sacrifice
for one another;

in the way of your Son
Jesus Christ our Lord,

Amen.

The God who will never forsake us

A prayer of thanksgiving to the God who will never forsake us.

We bless you, O God of all our life,
that you will never forsake us.
Even in our activity,
and restlessness,
and pace of our achieving lives,
you undergird us and hold us in being
although we don't want you,
and confidently declare you redundant.

It was not always so.

When we were children
you knocked on the wide door of our small hearts
and we were one with you in the play of life.
But we grew up and decided to put you away;
we needed to manage, you see, on our own.
So your presence faded,
the knock became a distant echo,
and when you tried to remind us of your presence
we resisted you,
our minds too full of projects,
our hearts of fantasies,
our souls of ambitions.
No room for you,
outcast God.

And you waited.

And then in our fragile vulnerability,
through pain
or the passing question of mortality,
doubt,
like a saviour visited us,
and found a crack in the hard shell of our certainties;
and the light of your truth
entered our emptiness.
And we cried out.

And you were still there.

And you found the child's heart within us,
still faintly beating;
and you breathed your peace upon us,
and we believed again,
and lived.

Blessed are you, O God of all our life, who will never forsake us.

The grace of music

Holy God,
who calls us beyond
the limits of our poor understandings,
and holds wide heaven's door
to receptive hearts,

take us in this holy place,
we pray,
by the grace of music,
into the wonder that silences all agitation,
into the praise that knits up all fear.

And lead us on
by the way of music
to glimpse a oneness
which cannot yet be fully seen,
and find a rest
which cannot yet be fully known.

So shall we perceive
that unity
which foreshadows the end of all divisions,
and that silence
which heralds the beginning of all joys;

and know ourselves to be, at last,
your redeemed people;

graced,
and raised
by song.

Amen.

The heart's true home

God our Keeper,
Shepherd of the trembling heart,
Guardian of the fragile soul,
and bearer of peace
to the chattering mind.

Pity us
in our agitations,
confusions,
and turmoil;

and draw us back,
gentle Father,
to our hearts' true home
from the far country of fantasy and desire
where we are for ever straying.

And in the strength of your understanding,
the embrace of your acceptance,
and the knowledge of our true belonging,
hold us safely,
frail children of fear,
in that place of your love
which is rest
and life
and peace;

even the heart of Jesus Christ
our Lord.

Amen.

The journey of faith

We bless you,
O God,
for our own faith journey.

For stumbling beginnings,
for confident certainties,
for the blessings of doubt,
for discoveries in darkness,
for shared questions,
for new ways of seeing,
for understandings stumbled on in unexpected places;

and for your grace accompanying us all the way,
hidden,
absent,
cried out for,
yet nearer than breathing.

O Divine Life-giver,
Pain-bearer,
Soul-maker,
keep us moving on;

and teach us each day
the ways of your dying,
that we may know in our disbelieving hearts
the power of your rising;
until the Day dawns
when we shall see you
face to face,
in Jesus Christ
our Lord.

Amen.

The Prodigal

Luke 15:11–32

God our Father,
as we reflect
on this extraordinary story of grace,
we offer to you
the hurt and pain of our damaged lives
and our constant need
of your healing.

O God,
we recognise only too well

our arrogant self-sufficiency,
mirrored in the younger son;

our moralistic self-righteousness,
mirrored in the older son;

our muddle and alienation,
mirrored in the pig-sty;

and our longing to return,
mirrored in the long, long road home.

Ever merciful God,
as we delight in the images
of the running father,
the welcoming embrace,
the tears of affection,
and the huge celebratory banquet,
keep us always
trusting in your acceptance,

and never afraid.

For your joy's sake.

Amen.

The Sower

A sower went out to sow . . .
some seed fell on the hard path . . .
some fell on rocky ground . . .
some fell among thorns . . .
some fell into good soil.
Luke 8:5ff

Spirit of God
you know our hearts;
stony, distracted, shallow;
and our blindness to our predicament.

Awaken us, we pray;

where the heart has become hard,
unyielding in the face of need
and deaf to others' pain,
give compassion;

where the heart has become distracted,
seduced and consumed
by an idolatrous world,
give sorrow;

where the heart has become shallow,
cluttered by trivia
adrift amidst the world's noise,
give silence;

where the heart has become small,
its imagination lost
deadened by cynicism,
give hope;

so rooted again in your mercy,
and dwelling again in your love,
we shall find your life
growing within us;

bearing fruit for your glory.

Amen.

The wastelands of the heart

O gentle Christ,
look with your merciful pity,
upon the wastelands of our hearts;

the wearisome anxieties,
the persistent defensiveness,
the hidden violence,
the pervasive fear;

and teach us again to receive
in the place of our silent waiting
the gift of your gentle coming;

that your Life
which is ours,
but becomes lost
in the tangle of our soul's confusion,
may *be* ours
as we abide in you;

who are one with the Father
and the Holy Spirit
in an eternal Trinity of Love;

now and evermore,

Amen.

The Way

The Bible is best understood as the narrative of a
long journey in search of the Kingdom of God;
so it was that the early Christians described their faith as 'The Way'.

A Way which began with Abraham, father of faith,
who set out not knowing where he was going;

that Moses shaped,
walking to freedom;

that the prophets pointed to,
insisting on justice;

that the Baptist prepared,
calling for repentance;

that Jesus re-fashioned,
in the self-giving of God;

that Andrew, Peter, and Paul followed,
even to death;

and that John revealed leads to heaven wide open,
with Christ the Ladder guiding us home.

O God, this Way
we too,
in our time,
seek to tread.

Strengthen our steps as we go;

when the road gets narrow and we falter,
hold us;
when it seems to disappear altogether and we doubt,
keep us;
when distractions claim our gaze and we turn away,
warn us;
and when we dare to trust your love and come near,
still us;

and so prepare us
for that vision of your glory
which is more than mind can embrace
or heart comprehend;

but is our Life,

in Jesus Christ our Lord.

Amen.

The wings of faith

We bless you,
God our Father,
for the gift of faith;

for the impulse
planted deep in all hearts
to launch out;
and trusting, beyond fear,
and risking beyond knowledge,
to find life . . .

We bless you
for the faith of children
who stretch out arms,
and find comfort . . .

for the faith of lovers
who surrender hearts,
and find fulfilment . . .

for the faith of artists,
who explore visions,
and find beauty . . .

for the faith of believers
who embrace darkness,
and find light . . .

O God, give us too
the wings of faith . . .

and widen their span
in our trembling
cramped hearts;

that in trust,
O God,
we may stretch;

and risking,
find joy.

Amen.

Thomas

We bless you,
O God,
for Thomas;

who mirrors our doubts,
echoes our questions,
and reflects our fear
that our minds are deluded
as we cling to faith
in a world that has forgotten you.

And then Christ comes to him and says:
'touch . . . see . . . believe . . .'
and
'blessed are those who do not see,
and yet believe'.

O Christ,
as those pronounced 'blessed'
we offer you
the incredulity of our minds,
the bewilderment of our hearts,
and ask
that you would come to us too
in the barren depths of our souls
where the doors are so often locked.

Come to us
we pray,
and fill us too
with your confidence and wonder and adoration;

that we may also
like Thomas
exclaim
– your life bursting from within us –

'My Lord and my God!'

Amen.

Travelling wayfaring God

Travelling, wayfaring God,
amidst the Babel of this world's confusion
your Spirit calls us to journey with your Son
as our reference point,
light,
and companion on the way.

As day by day we set out anew,
inspire us;

when we falter and fail,
hold us;

if we turn aside,
prevent us;

when we lose the path,
direct us;

and when the heart is ensnared by doubt
and the journey itself seems an illusion,
strengthen us;

that glimpsing signs of your love along the way,
the desert of our fear
may blossom like the rose;

and the dry ground of our need
gush forth,

with the springs of the water of life.

Amen.

Trinity

God, our Creator,
author of life,
architect of the universe
shaper of stars
lover of this earth, our home,

we worship you.

God, our Redeemer,
reaching into our forsakenness,
bloodied Man of Nazareth
stretched on a cross
for the world's freedom,

we worship you.

God, our Sanctifier,
fire of Life,
interpreter,
uniter, healer,
revealer of the Son,

we worship you.

Holy Triune God,
Father, Son and Spirit,
in the smallness of our vision,
the coldness of our love,
and the dullness of our hearts,
lift up our eyes;

that we may glimpse your glory
beyond our fears,
and your love
beyond our minds,

and be transformed in praise;
from glory to glory.

Amen.

Unknowing
(in the season of Christmas and Epiphany)

*The mystical tradition of the Church teaches that God is unknowable
and we must learn to wait in darkness for his coming.*

O infinite Mystery,
we bow before you
in awe and silence.

You are God;
beyond all words,
all names,
all understandings.

In ourselves,
we cannot find you;

and yet without you
our world is lost and empty
and we can only wait
in the longing of our night.

And yet in the darkness
you have revealed yourself;
as a rejected infant
to whom poor men were led
and wise men came with gifts.

As we see them kneel,
adoring,
the desire of their searching hearts satisfied,
teach us to follow in the same way;

and seeking,
to find

and finding
to know

and knowing
to find our longing ended.

Amen.

Unknowing

One of the early Fathers of the Church wrote:
'It is that perfect unknowing
that constitutes the true knowing
of the one who transcends all knowing.'
Dionysius the Areopagite

O infinite Mystery,
we bow before you
in awe and silence.

You are God
beyond all words,
all names,
all understandings.

In ourselves, we cannot find you
and yet without you
our world is lost and empty
and we can only wait
in the longing of our night.

And yet in the darkness
you have revealed yourself
as a rejected infant to whom poor men were led;
as a son of Man with nowhere to lay his head;
as a victim on a cross despised and rejected of men.

Open our eyes,
O outcast God,
to the unexpected ways of your coming;

and give us hearts to see you,
and courage to make you welcome;

that the darkness of our night
may be illumined like the dawn;

and our despair turned to song.

For your glory's sake.

Amen.

Waiting

We wait for your loving kindness, O God,
in the midst of your temple.
Psalm 48:9

God of the long day
and the silent hours of the night,
we find it so hard to wait;

with our hunger for results,
our need for recognition,
and innumerable fears driving us,
we find it so hard to wait;

and in a world of instant communication
no longer know how to.

Have mercy upon us,
and in our shallow restless agitation
hold us still,
and take us down
below the noisy surface of our minds
into the silent depths
of hearts grown cold by neglect,
of spirits barren and empty.

And there,
in the wastelands of our souls
teach us to wait for you;

and waiting, to find,
and finding, to adore,

in the midst of your Temple,

God our glory.

Amen.

Two

Prayers of Seeking the Kingdom of God

Addiction

He rebuked the wind and said to the sea,
'Peace, be still.'
Mark 4:39

God our healer,
have compassion on all who find themselves
enslaved to addictions
and overwhelmed by compulsions
that threaten their end;

all in whom
the image of your loveliness
has been buried and lost
in the hard ground of
a tormented heart.

Give strength to those who work with them,
and through the power of acceptance,
the skill of medical care,
and the suffering patience of friendship,
give,
we pray,
the priceless gift of freedom.

So may the tempestuous storm of need
be calmed,

and blessed peace
finally come.

For your love's sake.

Amen.

All Saints

Today is the Feast of All Saints,
when we bless God
for all those countless men and women,
known and unknown who have revealed the Image of God,
and become icons of Christ in their time,
shining like lights in a dark and murky world.

God our strength,
down the ages
the treasure of your presence
has been revealed
in the earthen vessels
of frail men and women who,
following the way of the Cross
have let go of their self-seeking,
waited in darkness,
and in the gift of a new identity,
found themselves.

Nourish in us those qualities
that have lit up their lives;

compassion, courage, humility, hope
and the capacity always to forgive;

so may we
on our pilgrimage
follow their steps;

and being formed
in Christ's likeness
bring to a troubled world
the healing of his peace.

For your joy's sake.

Amen.

Anxiety

God our healer,
who walked upon the chaotic waters
and said to the storm: 'Be still',
you know the failty of our hearts,
how easily anxiety can overwhelm us.

It lurks in the shadows of the mind,
spreads its coils around us,
throttles life within us,
and shuts the door of our generous hearts.

God our Saviour,
set us free
we pray
from the curse and burden of anxiety;
and by the miracle of your grace
show us how
perfect love casts out fear.

For your love's sake.

Amen.

Bethlehem

Pray for the city of Bethlehem.

The city where
under the silent stars
the hopes and fears
of all the years met;

Bethlehem

still silent at night,
its people under curfew now,
hemmed in,
afraid;

Bethlehem

where,
O God,
as a helpless infant
threatened by violence
you clung to life;

Bethlehem

city of fear,
where the world's salvation
dawned
in a child's cry;

O God
have mercy
upon the children of Bethlehem;

and there,
once again,

let hope be cradled.

Amen.

Cancer

Compassionate God
whose love in Christ
has embraced
the depths of our need;
look with mercy
on all whose lives have been traumatised
by cancer.

In their struggle
hold them,
we pray,
in the power of your life;
and draw them through all they experience –

darkness and light,
hope and desolation,
fear and pain –

into your loving embrace;

that they may be sustained
in the dark valley which they walk,
and come to know
in their trembling hearts
your never failing care
from which nothing
in life or death can separate us.

In Jesus Christ our Lord.

Amen.

Christ our King

*The Ascension of Christ is summed up
in the simplest of creeds, 'Jesus Christ is Lord',
whose meaning is revealed in the lives of the saints.*

A prayer for a world estranged from the Lordship of Christ:

Christ our King,
amid the confusion of
warring gods
and seductive idolatries
that delude
men and women
in a world estranged from you,
you alone are Lord.

Down the centuries
your life
has lit up the lives of the saints
who have shone like lights in the dark.

Through simplicity and sacrifice,
humility and joy,
they have revealed
the freedom of your peace,
and called to a world
lost
in the far country of its exile.

Open our eyes
in our time,
we pray,
to the extent of our alienation;

free us from the tyranny of our pleasure-seeking
and kindle within us too
a longing to return to the way of holiness;

so may we also
know the gift of your joy,

and our lives too
shine with the light of your love.

For your joy's sake.

Amen.

Come and see

As his Gospel begins, John the evangelist
invites his readers to 'Come and see';
to have their sight purified,
their eyes opened,
so they may catch a glimpse of the vision of God
and be healed.

So amidst the confusion and conflicts of our world, we pray:

O Christ,
Light of the world
and giver of light to the blind,
look with mercy upon your world darkened
in the limitations of our perceptions,
the distortions of our prejudices
and the anguish of our conflicts.

O merciful Saviour,
again and again
our vision is clouded,
our sight partial,
and what we see
in the face of others
is not your image
but the projection of our fear.

O crucified Lord,
as we gaze upon your cross
open our eyes to your love for us
even as we crucify your image in one another;

and as we see,
teach us to repent;

and repenting
to embrace;

that embracing our enemy
we may find ourselves healed,

in your forgiveness
and endless peace.

Amen.

Darkness

God has said he would dwell in thick darkness (Psalm 18:11)
and to him darkness and light are both alike (Psalm 139:12).

A prayer for all who know their susceptibility
to the power of irrational anxieties and fears.

We remember before you,
Comforter God,
all those who understand
only too well
the fragility of their own minds;
who know how easily they can be overwhelmed
by irrational terrors
over which they feel they have little control.

And we pray for the courage
not to turn away
from the long shadows of our own hearts,
the forbidding familiar darknesses of our own fears
that can besiege us suddenly
in the depths of the night
and suggest not your presence,
loving Father,
but blackest night
and absence.

Teach us,
O Christ,
who was crucified in darkness,
and descended into hell
how it is
that darkness and light
to you are both alike?

Teach us how,
even in the night
you are somehow still our friend?

Teach us
even as we cry to you
and hear nothing,
how it can be
that in and through
that which most terrifyingly overshadows
there is the promise that we shall find
the miracle of your joy?

O Holy One, O Comforter, O Saviour of all,
teach us we pray,

and bring us peace.

Amen.

Emmaus

In the resurrection, Christ comes again to us
even as we are in despair over the violence of our world –
our prejudices, hatreds, and the depths of our divisions;

he comes as one who is strange and foreign
and walks beside us
and invites us to see him.

O Christ
who walks beside us on the road
unrecognised,
unknown,
and unbelieved in,

you know the despair that violence brings,
the bitterness of its pain,
and our inability to break out
of the prison house of its repetition.

O Holy One
whose body was broken by our hatreds
and yet who would still be guest of all our hearts,
abide with us as darkness falls
we pray,
and kindle again within us
the fire of your reconciling love;

and as the bread of our certainties is broken
give us grace to see you
beyond our divisions;

and recognise your image, O Lord,

in the face of the stranger.

Amen.

God of the poor

God of mercy and judgement,
whose heart burns with love
for the poor and outcast.

In your Son Jesus Christ,
you bring
sight to the blind,
release for captives,
and freedom for the oppressed.

Strengthen the hearts of your children
ensnared in injustice
in a world cruelly divided
between rich and poor.

Father,
bring comfort where there is loss,
courage where there is fear,
hope where there is despair,
and,
persevering in the way of your cross,
glimpses of your kingdom
coming on this earth,

where you were crucified in pain,
and rose in glory.

Amen.

Grief

Crucified and risen Lord
you know the grief of our hearts
the pain of our loss
the agony we share.

Have mercy upon us
in our frailty and sorrow,
and teach us that
deeper than our fears
the power of your love
is constant and abiding,
stronger than loss and death.

Nourish this faith,
we pray,
constantly within us;

and so renew in us day by day
a firm step,
a bright hope,
and in the confidence of your mercy
a joyful disposition,

that amidst all the tribulations of the world
we may yet be diffusers of life;
by the power of your Spirit,
and in the name of Jesus Christ.

Amen.

Grieving God

Grieving sorrowful God,

who wept at Bethany
at the grave of Lazarus,

who shuddered in fear
in the garden of Gethsemane,

and shared at Golgotha
the desolation of death,

draw near we pray
to those whose sorrowing at this time
takes them into a pit of forsakenness
where darkness overwhelms.

Be to them,
we pray,
light in their travail
presence in their struggle
and
strength in their fear;

that from the ashes of their dereliction
may come the sweet comfort of hope.

In the name of Jesus Christ
our risen Lord.

Amen.

Homes and families

We bless you,
Lord our God,
for homes and families
which reflect the way of Jesus Christ.

For homes
where parents listen to children,
couples serve one another,
children take risks,
all dare to be vulnerable,
and strangers are welcomed.

O God
give us homes where

the beauty of your humanity
is shaped

and the loveliness of your image
is revealed.

For your love's sake.

Amen.

John the Baptist

A voice crying in the wilderness:
'Prepare the way of the Lord,
make his paths straight.'
Luke 3:4

We bless you
God our Saviour,
for the courage of John,
forerunner of your Christ.

As we hear again
the hard simplicity of his proclamation
look with mercy upon us
in our captivity to so much that is false in our world:

our fascination with image,
our skill in fabrication,
our manipulation of truth.

Father,
in the midst
of so much unreality
give your people courage
to walk
the hard way of holiness and integrity

and discover,
in surprise,

the road to freedom.

Amen.

Joseph of Nazareth

Today we remember Joseph of Nazareth.

Joseph, the carpenter,
descendant of David;

Joseph, man of dreams,
and husband of Mary;

Joseph, carer and role model
of the child
who was the Christ.

We bless you,
Lord our God,
for your servant Joseph;
who taught the heart of the young boy he cared for
the meaning of the word 'Abba';
and nourished in the growing child
the tender shoots of a faith
that would light up the world.

Give us the same
patient faith,
diligent watching,
and abiding trust,
as we exercise our responsibilities
in the care and nurture of young people.

And fashion in us too
a heart
big enough to stand aside
and rejoice,

when we see the dawning of your glory,
O God,
in the life of a child.

Amen.

Judgement

God of majesty and glory
we are afraid of the power of judgement
seen in cataclysmic ways in our world;

in the anguish of divided nations,
the disorders of the natural world,
and the blindness of our violence
our sins are laid frighteningly bare.

Have mercy on us;
and wake us up to
the depth of
our alienation,
disobedience
and faithlessness.

And lead us home,
O God,
from our bitter exile
into the way of your commandments
and the place of your forgiveness;
that our lives,
our homes,
and our world
may be filled with the knowledge of your love,

and your holy fear.

Amen.

King of kings

Blessed are you,
Lord Jesus Christ,
King of kings,
Lord of lords

whose crown was of thorns,
whose throne a cross,
who carried not a sceptre of royalty,
but the towel of a slave;

blessed are you
who amidst all posturings of power
revealed that Love is the undersong of the universe
whose notes will never die;

blessed are you who on the third day
opened eyes to see
that despite all betrayals,
in the end all shall be well;

blessed are you
who in the twilight of fear
gives strength to insist on justice,
courage to question power,
and wisdom to unveil meaning
in a world that has forgotten you;

blessed are you,
Lord Jesus Christ,
King of kings,
and Lord of lords.

Amen.

Love one another

O God,
through your Son
you have given the Church
a new commandment
of love for one another;

given not through fire and fear
on tablets of stone,
but with the towel of service
and the washing of feet
at the Passover table.

And we bless you that
what you commanded is possible
through your Spirit alive among us
ending fear,
breaking down walls,
and shaping
out of the scattered fragments
of a divided people
a single new humanity.

O God, as we kneel in service before
your image
hidden in one another,
transform us into
men and women who are no longer
at odds
or divided
or blind to one another's gifts,
but, belong together in love,
members of a single body,

so may we be an instrument of your peace
for the world's healing.

In the name of Christ,

Amen.

O Jerusalem, Jerusalem

'O Jerusalem, Jerusalem,' said Jesus,
'. . . How often have I longed to gather your children together
as a hen gathers her brood under her wings,
and you were not willing!' (Matthew 23:37);
'If only you knew on this day the things that make for peace
but they are hidden from your eyes . . .' (Luke 19:42).

Compassionate God,
our hearts are anguished
by the tragedy of your holy city,
the suffering of Palestinian and Israeli,
of Jew, Muslim and Christian.

In the peace of this holy place
we offer our prayers
for all whose lives are engulfed in violence.

O crucified Jesus,
Lamb of God,
who takes away the sin of the world,
strengthen the nerve
and sustain the faith of those
who work for an end to the destruction.

Teach them
those hidden things
that make for peace;
and even in this darkest night
bring nearer the Day of the New Jerusalem
when there shall be no more crying or lamentation in the street,
because the former things are passed away,
and in the reconciliation of your Son,
all things made new.

Amen.

One common humanity

There is no longer Jew or Greek,
slave or free, male or female;
for all of you are one in Christ Jesus.
Galatians 3:28

We give thanks for the promise of liberation
of all humankind in Christ
and the overcoming of divisions
of race, class or gender.

Liberating God,
have mercy upon your people
still divided and ensnared in prejudices

of race
that lead to violence;

of gender
that betray trust;

of class
that cause division.

And bring nearer that day
when in the diversity of our humanity

the fear of one another
is removed,

the potential of one another
is seen,

and the love of one another
is realised;

continued

so may we become in these islands
and our world
one common humanity;
rejoicing in difference
and held together in peace,

the peace given
through the way of the Cross

the Cross of Jesus Christ,
our Lord.

Amen.

Out of the depths

Out of the depths have I cried to you, O Lord.
Psalm 130:1

We remember this night
all who are in extreme situations
of despair,
of torture, loneliness, mental illness . . .

O most High God
who has descended
from the heights of heaven
down to the very depths,
even to the pit of death
and the abyss of forsakenness
where no light shines;

hear with your merciful ears
all who from a place of anguish
cry to you.

In your compassion
draw near to them,
O crucified God;

and by your wounds
calm their terror,
heal their pain,
and bring them out
from a place of fear
to a land of hope,
where love lives again.

For your holy name's sake.

Amen.

Paul of Tarsus

We bless you,
O Lord our God,
for your servant
Paul,
whose terrible persecution of the Church
wonderfully collapsed
in the face of your risen Son,
and whose energy in Christ
took the message of grace
beyond Judaism
to the Gentile world.

As we glimpse
the depth of his sacrifice
and the fullness of his joy,
forgive the hesitant timidity
of our praise;

and nourish within us also
a faith like his,

wide enough
to embrace the world.

Amen.

Pray for the peace of Jerusalem

Pray for the peace of Jerusalem . . .

the city of God,
where the tribes go up
and the great faiths meet
and the children of Abraham
co-exist in fear;

Pray for the peace of Jerusalem . . .

where young Palestinians hurl their stones
young Israelis fire their bullets
and the mothers of them both
bury their dead;

Pray for the peace of Jerusalem . . .

for the Jew beseeching at the wailing wall,
for the Muslim bowing in the Al Aksa Mosque,
for the Christian walking the narrow uphill way
of the Via Dolorosa;

Pray for the peace of Jerusalem . . .

Father of Abraham,
have mercy upon your warring children
Jew, Muslim, and Christian;
and in your mercy reveal to us
those hidden things that make for peace;
that the night may end
and the day dawn that leads
to the New Jerusalem,
that city which is your gift to all people where

continued

love transcends divisions,
forgiveness destroys barriers,
mercy heals wounds,
and peace finally triumphs,

because you are God.

We ask it in the name of the crucified and risen One,
Jesus Christ.

Amen.

The alienated heart

Break down,
O Lord my God,
the stony wall of fear
that keeps me locked away
cold,
separate,
alone,
sealed in my own
unyielding suspicion.

Dead,
as the apostle said,
in sin.

Give me the confidence
to prise open
the small door
of my vulnerable heart
and risk another's entry.

Let me find that inner place
of risk and trust
where my heart,
softened
by the understanding of another's gaze,
may belong again;

and leaving behind its frozen isolation
be warmed;

and in a shared life,
find the gift of joy.

Amen.

The brink of war

We offer to God our anguish
and fear for our world
as clouds of war gather,
prejudices harden,
judgements are made,
violence embraced.

God our Father,
you have created humankind
to be one community
of diverse peoples on the face of the earth,
and have called us to love one another.

Have mercy upon us
in the depth of our divisions
and the poison of our hatreds.

Forgive our blinkered vision,
the things we defend,
the things we ignore,
our idolatries,
our secret love of violence,
and our refusal to search for a better way.

Strengthen the hearts of those
who
even as darkness falls
yet strive to build bridges of peace
across widening chasms of mistrust.

In the name of Jesus Christ,
the Prince of Peace.

Amen.

The coming of God

God is both the Comforter
who comes with the gift of rest,
and the One who promises to come
with the gift of hope.

We are called, paradoxically,
both to rest in his love
and to keep awake for his coming.

Comforting hopeful God,
you who are
calm to the bewildered,
rest to the weary,
and healing to the broken,

so ground our wayward hearts
in the knowledge of your love,
that resting in your peace
we may wake from the sleep of death
drifting over a faithless world.

Teach us the extent of our betrayal;
and in the night-time of our neglect
keep us watchful for your coming
and alert to receive
the light of your Son

in whose dawning brightness
we shall see,

and in whose gathering strength
we shall trust.

Amen.

The cruelty of life

We remember all who feel beaten
by what can seem like the random cruelty of life.

Those numbed by the sudden news of redundancy
and unemployment;
or the sudden onset of terminal illness;
or who feel hollowed out by the experience of bereavement
and face the world in all its business and indifference alone,
having lost someone they love.

We remember any who struggle in a dark place.

O God,
in Jesus Christ,
you have entered the pit of our sorrows,
have shared in the cruelty of life's injustice,
and with us have lain in the tomb.

Embrace,
with your compassion
we pray,
all who carry burdens of loss or pain or sorrow
that are too heavy for them.

Especially we remember . . .

Sustain them in their darkness,
and keep them
enduring in hope
that the night will end,
day will dawn,
and you will be there.

Blessed are you
who suffered in our night,
and comes with the dawning of the day.

In Jesus Christ
our Lord.

Amen.

The elderly and those who live alone

*A prayer for those who live alone,
or who especially feel the frailty of their life:*

O God,
when my mind is overwhelmed by fear,
have mercy on me;

when my spirit is wasted by loneliness,
have mercy on me;

when my heart is choked by grief
and the memory of those I have loved and lost,
have mercy on me;

when my soul is full of questioning doubt about the meaning
of my life
and whether I am of any use to anybody any more,
have mercy on me.

Come to me,
O Lover of souls;
save me from self-pity and despair,
renew in me a deeper trust,
and take me to yourself this night,
and every night
until the end of my life shall come,
and I shall rest in you for ever.

In Jesus Christ our Lord.

Amen.

The face of Christmas

The Word became flesh and dwelt among us . . .
John 1:14

As we kneel in this holy place,
we bless you,
Lord our God,
for the gift of one another this Christmas time.

We bless you
for all that we have experienced in our homes
and all that we are to one another;

for hopes shared and understandings given,
for stories told and love received,
for pain expressed and forgiveness offered,
belonging celebrated and joy found;

and we remember all for whom Christmas
is a time of anguish and dread,
through bereavement, loss,
depression, or violence.

Father,
as we step forward into a New Year,
strengthen our resolve
to let Christ
shape the pattern of our lives
form the habits of our hearts
heal our wounds
and guide our steps,

that in a dark world
we may reveal
the light of his face.

For his joy's sake.

Amen.

The faith of Abraham

*Abraham is the father of faith for
Jews, Muslims and Christians.*

We pray for a faith like his.

God,
who ever calls us into the new,
give us the faith of him
who left the settled routines of a
familiar world
and in obedience
to your call
set out,
not knowing where he was going.

Give us such faith on our journeying;
and as we leave the familiar
explore different insights
and risk new beginnings,
take us,
O God of surprises
into paths of understanding
now beyond our imagining.

And as we travel
give us the gift of
a new respect
for the faith of those
beside us on the road,
who also call Abraham
'Father'.

In the name of him
who loved the world,

Jesus Christ,
our Lord.

Amen.

The forgotten children

*'Let the little children come to me . . .
for it is to such as these that the kingdom of heaven belongs.'*
Matthew 19:14

God our Father,
hear the cry of our hearts for
the forgotten children of the world;
who through war, abuse, poverty, or AIDS
cannot be children.

The children of the West Bank towns
imprisoned under curfew;

the child soldiers of rag-tag armies in Africa
whose toys are real guns;

the children who through AIDS
suddenly must be parents
because they have none.

Father, so many children –
their innocence violated,
minds traumatised,
childhood lost,
their dreams nightmares.

O God
forgive us our neglect,
and strengthen our resolve
to promote
the justice that will guard innocence,
the freedoms that will enable play.

For your love's sake,

Amen.

The mentally ill

O Christ,
who cast out demons
and had compassion on the demoniac
whose name was legion,
you know the fragility of our minds;

how easily our hearts
are flooded by irrational fears;

our souls overshadowed
by half-remembered traumas;

our spirits weakened
by memories we thought we had banished,
but lie buried in the dungeon of the psyche
where they wreak their silent revenge.

Have compassion on those
who when the night of their fear
looms within them
lose the ground of their mind
and are overwhelmed.

O Crucified God,
in their terror
stay with them,
and lead them to trust
your gift of acceptance
given in the embrace and skill
of understanding friends;

so may they find
the hope they cannot see
yet cling to blindly
in the faith
that you are God,

and promise
the miracle of light,
and laughter,
and freedom dawning.

Amen.

The prison of war

O God who wept over Jerusalem,
look with compassion
on all who are locked
in the dark prison house of war
especially in . . .

We pray for all
whose minds have become captive to brutality,
and whose hearts are deadened by violence
in a cause
that in their dreams seemed noble,
but in the chaos of conflict
and the calculation of killing
has become base,
as your image in their enemy is forgotten.

God of hope,
the ultimate victory of love
cannot fail.

Come with your truth and light;

strengthen the peace-makers;

and in the places of our world
where your body is crucified again
turn the night-time of our violence
into the day-break of your reconciliation;

so may we find,
O God,
hope renewed,
faith vindicated,
and peace finally reborn.

Blessed are you
God of the Easter morning
who,
beyond hatred and death,

comes with the rising Son.

Amen.

The question why

O mysterious Origin of all Life,
Ground of Being,
we wonder at the miracle of our existence;

that out of the chaos of the fiery beginning
and the long turmoil of evolution
we, frail humans,
have emerged,
our vision dazzled by our consciousness,
and you have planted in our hearts
the question
'why?'

God of the searching heart,
God of the exploring mind,
God of the questioning spirit,
lead us on
into an ever deeper understanding
of this universe,
our home,
and our purpose within it.

And teach us through all we find along the way
to know and see you more clearly
to love and worship you more dearly
to follow and obey you more nearly
until our questioning hearts are finally won;

and we come home to the meaning of our lives
revealed in your Son
who is Lord of all,
Jesus Christ.

Amen.

The search for God

All praying is a search for the Mystery of God
infinite, beyond all comprehending,
yet nearer than breathing.

O loving Mystery of God
revealed in the face of Jesus Christ,

in all the circumstances of our lives
our search for you,
conscious and unconscious,
never ends.

In darkness and pain	we seek you.
In silence and beauty	we seek you.
In the sorrow of repentance and the trust of faith	we seek you.
In the face of the stranger and the welcome of a friend	we seek you.
In the horror of war and the cry for peace	we seek you.
In the wounds of our neighbour and action for justice	we seek you.
In the speaking of truth and the breaking of bread	we seek you.

O Mystery of God
infinitely far,
intimately near,
teach us how to seek you:

empty us of our self-sufficiency
give us eyes to see and ears to hear,
and so, gently disciplined
in the school of poverty and silent trust,
may we find you,

and finding you, love you,

and loving you, know ourselves
reborn

in joy and freedom.

Amen.

Those in prison

We pray for those in prison,
for those who wait for trial,
and all who suffer in situations of domestic violence.

Compassionate God,
we remember before you
all who are imprisoned behind bars
or trapped in destructive habits
of violence and fear.

We remember especially

those whose upbringing was so scarred
they have no patience to wait;

whose homes were so violent
they have no strength to endure;

whose childhood was so abused
they know only the language of abuse.

Lord God,
in your Son
you entered the hard brutality of our world
and with your arms outstretched upon a cross
you suffered it.

Have mercy upon those consumed
in cycles of violence
whose origins they cannot comprehend;

and breathe,
O Spirit of Love,
into damaged souls
the healing of your peace
opening the possibility of another way;

not of weakness and violence
and fear,

but of strength and integration
and peace.

In the name of Christ the healer.

Amen.

Unity

Through Christ
God was pleased to reconcile all things,
whether in heaven or on earth . . .
Colossians 1:20

God our Father,
in your Son Jesus Christ
you are wonderfully drawing
all things into one.

We bless you for signs of your purpose
dawning in our world;

for marriages and homes
who know the beauty of unity of heart;

for colleagues at work
who rejoice in unity of purpose;

for friends of different faiths
who celebrate unity of understanding;

for countries scarred by war
who have found unity in peace.

And we bless you
for those moments when,
across divisions,
we have had the grace
to listen to those with whom we disagree
to see afresh another's view
to struggle again with our own perceptions
and by the power of your Spirit
to break through disagreements,
and become one.

Keep us, we pray, in search
of this precious,
hard-won gift of unity;

that rejoicing in diversity
we may yet draw ever closer
to that coming Day
when in Christ Jesus

all things will be one.

For his glory's sake.

Amen.

Whole ministry

God our Father and Mother,
you call men and women
to serve together
in the proclamation of your gospel
to an unbelieving world.

We bless you for those women who have been
called into the ministry of your Church
to offer the praises of your people,
celebrate the mysteries of your love,
and proclaim the forgiveness of your grace.

Strengthen and encourage them
in the contribution they make;

that the heart of your Church may beat more tenderly,
the soul of your Church may listen more sensitively,
the mind of your Church may understand more deeply,
and the body of your Church may care more practically.

So, more whole and free
we shall rise up
and embrace with your Good News
the heart of all humanity
as we rejoice in the liberation of your Son,
our Saviour
Jesus Christ.

Amen.

Your Kingdom come

In the silence of this holy place,
I offer you,
O my God,
the longing of my anxious heart
for the miracle of peace in your world.

O crucified Christ,
who prayed from the Cross
'Forgive them for they know not what they do',
have mercy upon a world where
cruelty triumphs over mercy,
fanaticism destroys faith,
and terror becomes a means of persuasion.

And wherever men and women
bearing your image
are denied their humanity,
bring in your kingdom of justice;

that all may live
in the dignity of your freedom
and know the joy of your peace.

For your love's sake.

Amen.

Zeal

Following Jesus' cleansing of the Temple
his disciples remembered that it was written,
'Zeal for your house will consume me.'
John 2:17

Yet in our world we are only too conscious
of the awful dangers of zeal in matters of belief.

So we pray,
O God,
for all Christians, Muslims, Hindus or Jews
whose hearts are consumed
by a zeal that has hardened them;

all
whose vision is partial,
whose mind is narrowed,
whose perceptions are simplified,
whose soul is poisoned.

And yet,
O God,
we read of Jesus that
'zeal for your house consumed him'.

His life teaches us that
without the zeal of a burning love for you
that will endure through
the night-time of our enmities
we shall not see your kingdom come.

So we ask,
O God,
that you give us
a zeal that insists on acceptance
a commitment that endures in non-violence
and a patience that works for your coming;

and teach us to hate
only our tribalism and prejudice
which separate us
from those different to us.

We ask it in the name of the Prince of Peace,

Jesus Christ
our Lord,

Amen.

Index of Seasons

Index of Subjects